cultivate kindness

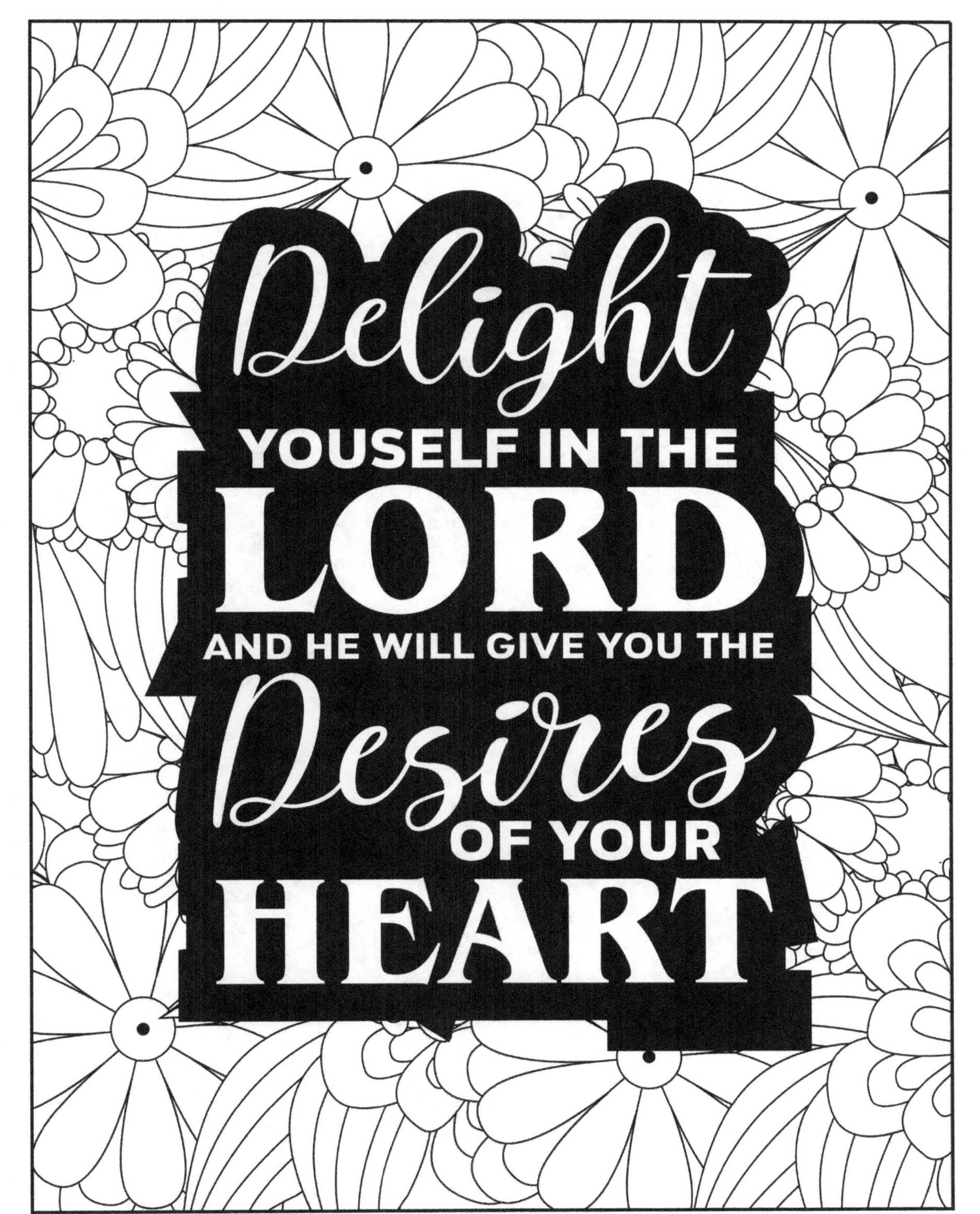
Delight
YOUSELF IN THE
LORD
AND HE WILL GIVE YOU THE
Desires
OF YOUR
HEART

CONTROL
YOUR
TEMPER
FOR ANGER
LABELS YOU A FOOL

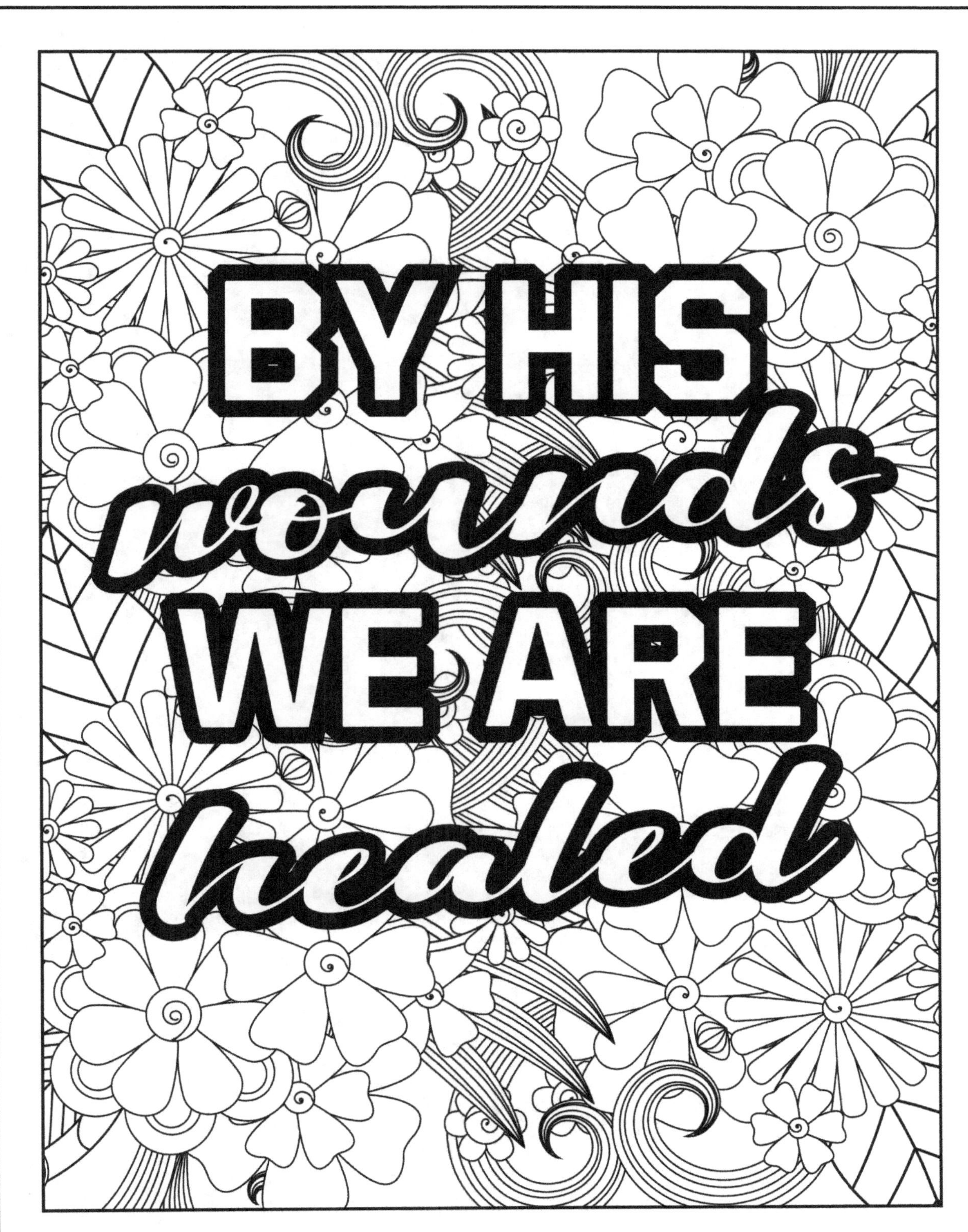

BY HIS
wounds
WE ARE
healed

CHRIST LIVES
IN ME

Blessed
IS THE ONE WHO
Trusts
IN THE
Lord

Be still
and know
that I am
GOD

ACT
JUSTLY
LOVE
MERCY
WAKE
HUMBLY

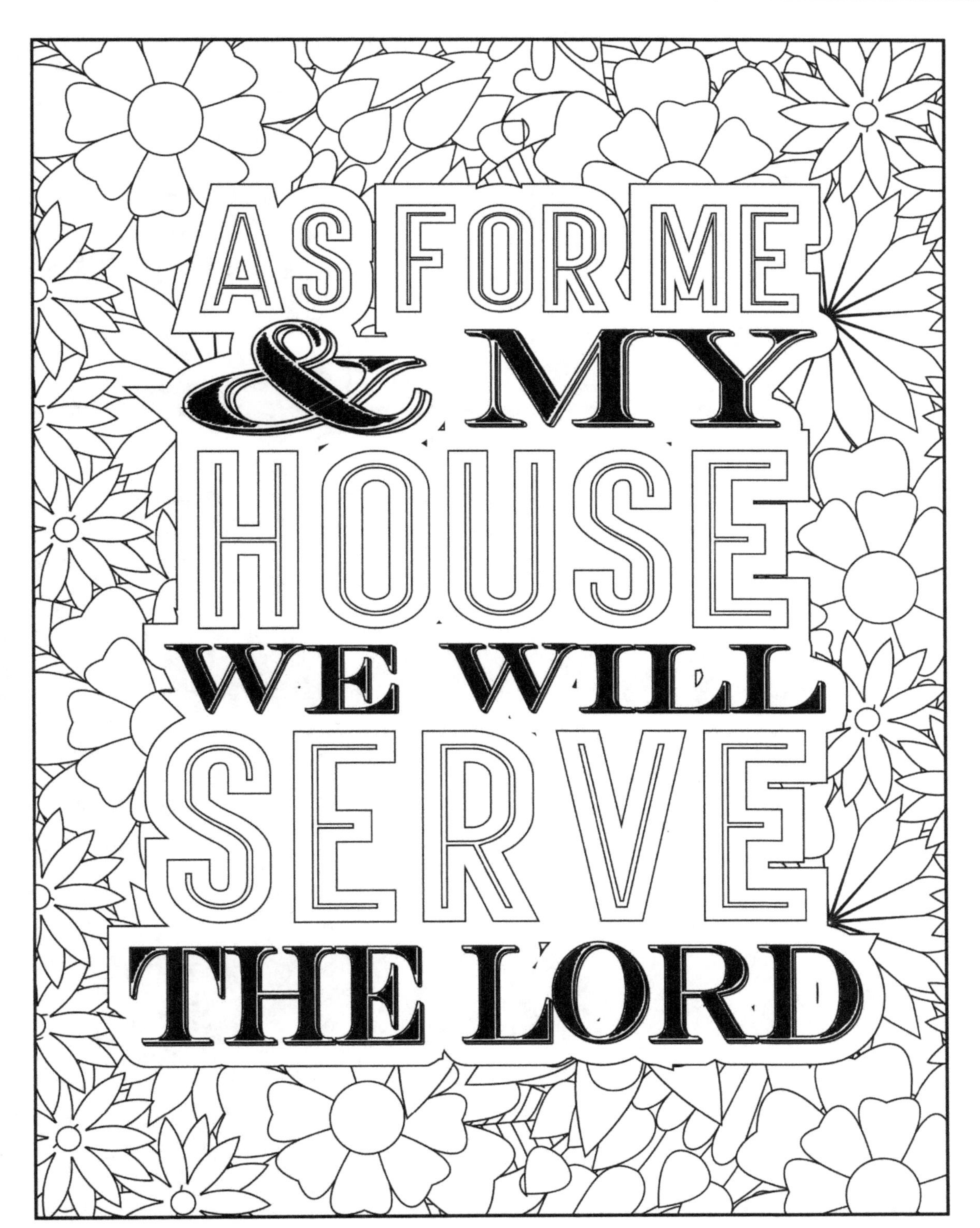

AS FOR ME
& MY
HOUSE
WE WILL
SERVE
THE LORD

IRON
SHARPENS
IRON
ONE
MAN
SHARPENS
ANOTHER

Pray
MORE
Worry
LESS

don't be
afraid
to be
Great

The
JOY
of the
LORD
is my
STRENGTH

JESUS
IS MY
BEST FRIEND

IN
Everything
GIVE
THANKS

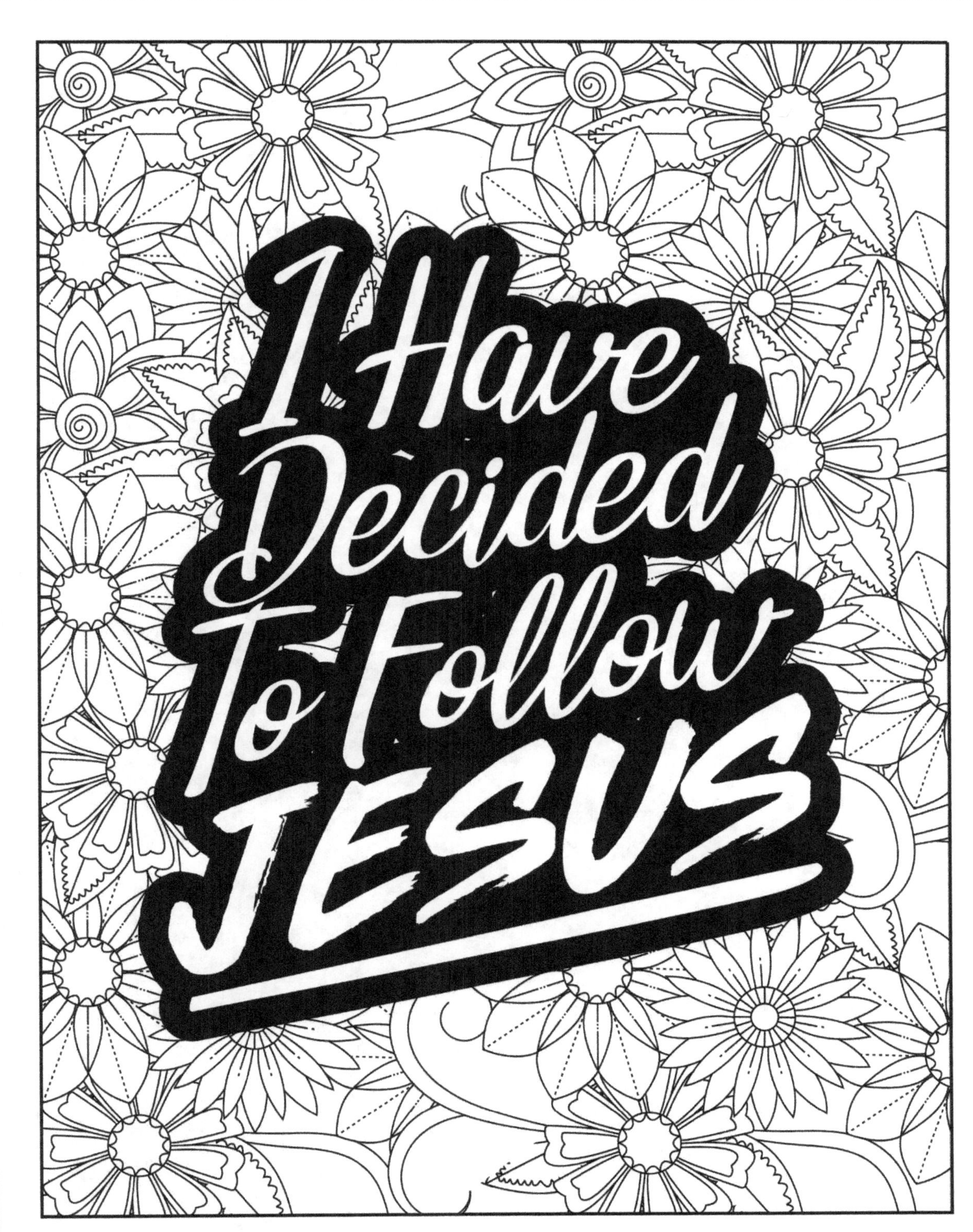

I Have Decided To Follow JESUS

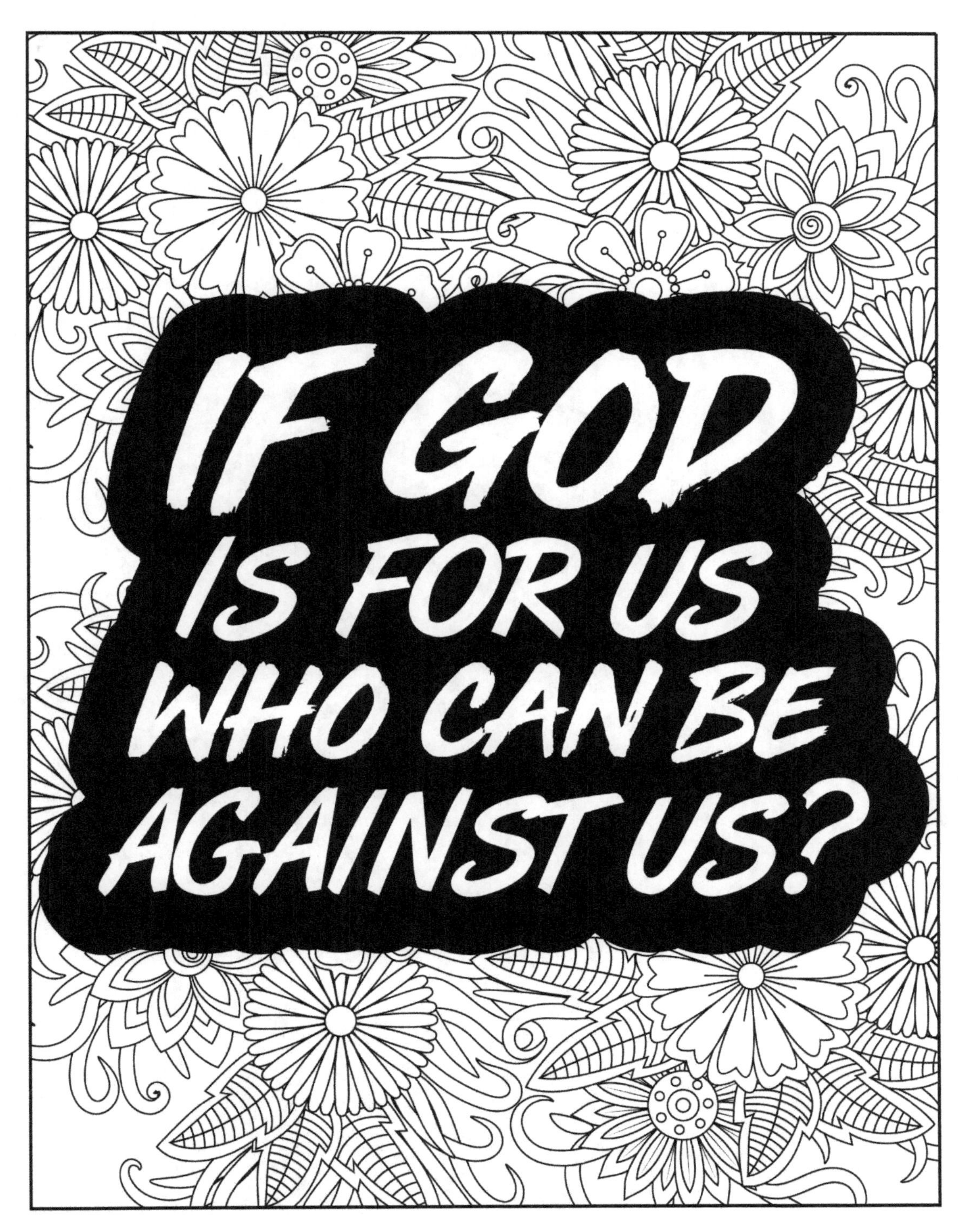

IF GOD IS FOR US WHO CAN BE AGAINST US?

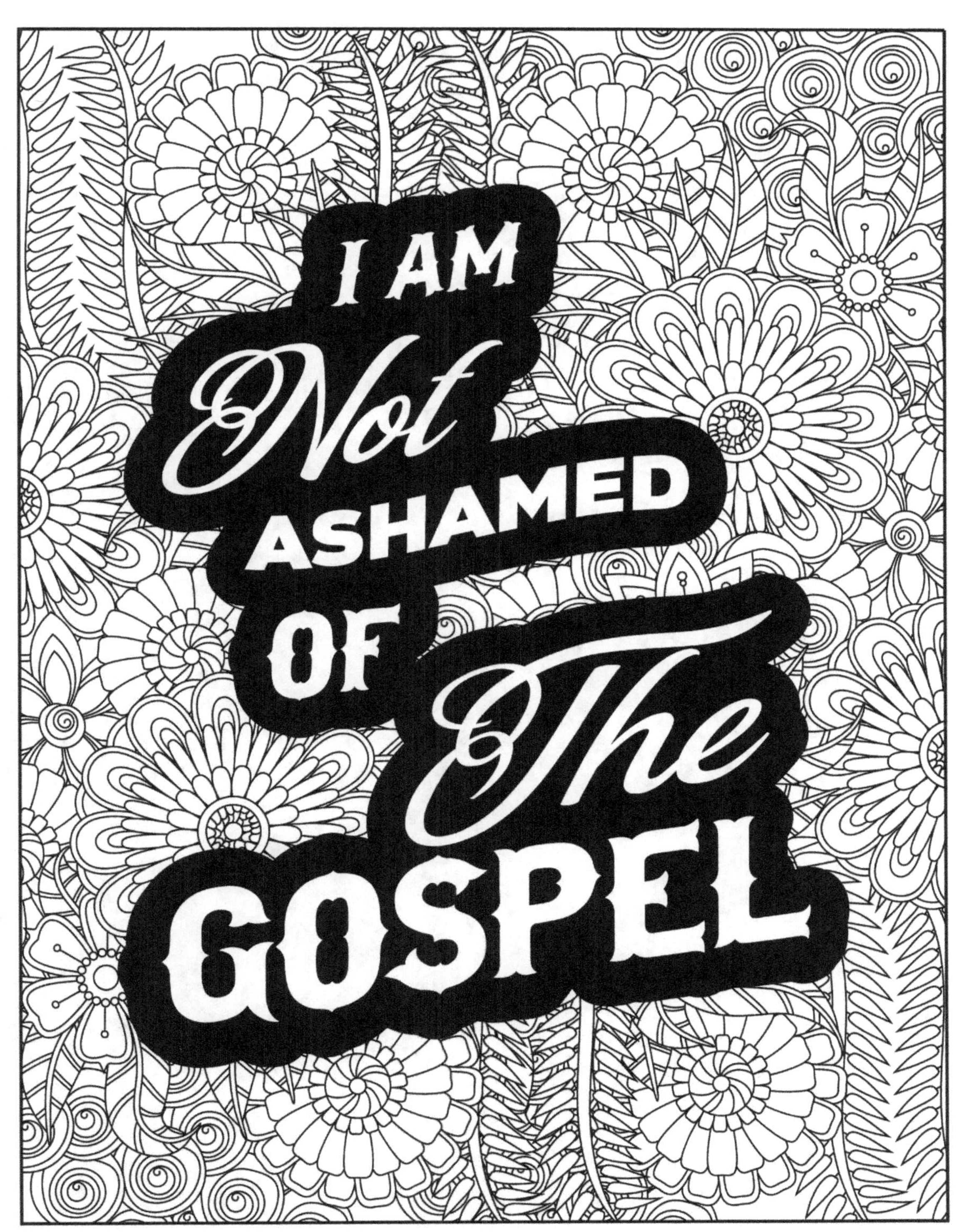

I AM
Not
ASHAMED
OF
The
GOSPEL

HONOR
GOD

Hope is
A
Waking
DREAM

FOR WITH
GOD
NOTHING
SHALL BE
IMPOSSIBLE

FIGHT
A GOOD FIGHT
FINISH
THE RACE
KEEP
THE FAITH

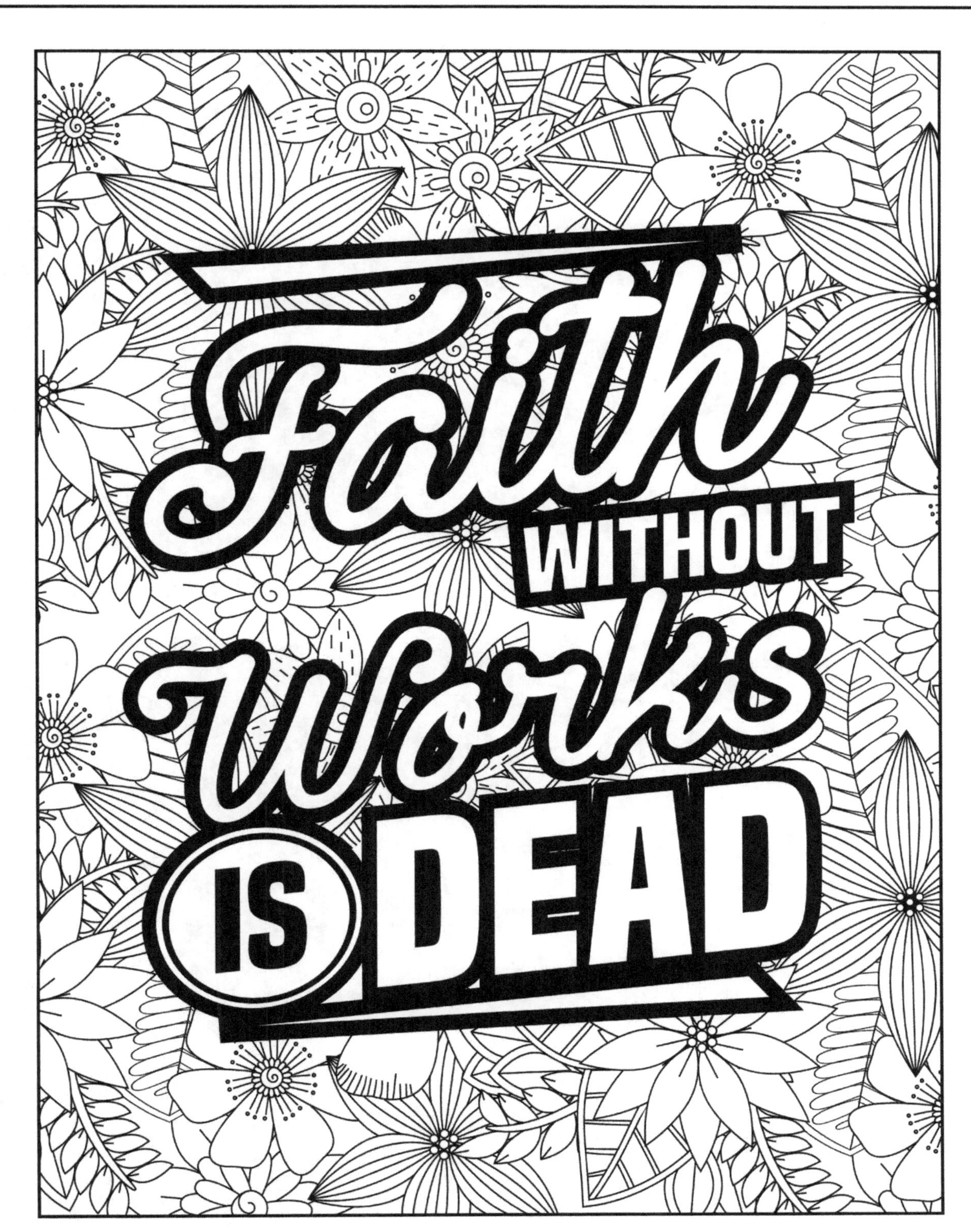

Faith
WITHOUT
Works
IS DEAD

Fearfully
AND
Wonderfully
MADE

Faith
★ OVER ★
Fear